FR. MIKE SC

IT'S PERSONAL

CULTIVATING YOUR RELATIONSHIP WITH GOD

ASCENSION

West Chester, Pennsylvania

Ascension
PO Box 1990
West Chester, PA 19380

1-800-376-0520
ascensionpress.com

Cover design: Rosemary Strohm

21 22 23 24 25 5 4 3 2 1

Printed in the United States of America
ISBN 978-1-950784-96-7

CONTENTS

Welcome to *The Curious Catholic*! Each booklet in this series is created to invite busy Catholics closer to God. Here Ascension offers you bite-sized discussions about important topics in day-to-day Catholic life. *The Curious Catholic* is designed to make it easy to fit spiritual growth into your day.

The booklets in this series are short and relatable with features that will help you apply what you read to your own life.*

Quotes and **Bible verses** throughout the booklets help you zero in on the key points.

Questions after each chapter prompt you to **reflect** and help you to dive deeper into the topic. We recommend praying or journaling with these questions as you make connections to your everyday life. The questions also make great prompts for small group discussion. Just keep in mind that not everyone in your group may feel comfortable answering the more personal questions.

Each chapter finishes with a challenge to **act**. These challenges invite you to enter into prayer, serve others, make a resolution for the week, and more.

We hope *The Curious Catholic* helps you along the way in your journey toward sainthood. May God bless you!

*Note: This booklet is adapted from a series of homilies given by Fr. Mike Schmitz.

Chapter 1

HOW TO PRAY

From the very first page to the very last page, the Bible tells a story. And there is one idea that sums up that entire story: the idea of covenant.

Now here's a little theology lesson—a covenant is different from a contract. Why? Because in a contract, the idea is that I'll do something for you, if you do something for me. It's an exchange of goods or services. But a covenant is an exchange of *persons*. In a covenant, you say, "I am yours, and you are mine."

The whole plan of God is to bring us into covenantal relationship. That's the theological term for what is going on here. So let's talk about it in our everyday language. It means that God's plan is to have a personal relationship with us.

And yet do you know that many Catholics are not absolutely convinced that it's possible to have a personal relationship with God?[1] But the whole story of the Bible is about that!

RELATIONSHIP

The Bible tells us how God enters into different covenants with his people as they wait for the Messiah. Then God fulfills all of those covenants in Jesus. At the Last Supper, Jesus says, "This is my blood of the covenant" (Matthew 26:28). So everything God does in the entire Bible is to bring us into covenant.

> EVERYTHING GOD DOES IN THE ENTIRE BIBLE IS TO BRING US INTO COVENANT.

Why did God establish covenants? So we could have a personal relationship with him. In Romans chapter 10, St. Paul talks about how God has justified us in Christ. Justified doesn't simply mean he redeemed us and saved us, although that's true. What it means is this: Jesus came so that we could have a personal relationship with God. Why did we get baptized? Although it's true that we got baptized so that we don't have to go to hell, there's more. We were baptized so that we could have a personal relationship with God. Why do we go to Mass? At Mass, we get fed by the Blood of Christ, the Blood of the new and eternal covenant, so that we can have a personal relationship with Jesus.

The whole Bible and everything we do as Catholics is about being brought into covenant, being brought into personal relationship with God. And yet many people reading this might not be certain that it's even possible to have a personal relationship with God.

NOTHING PERSONAL?

For many, going to Mass is nothing personal. We stand up when it's time for the Gospel—we hear those things and say, "Thanks be to God" or "Praise to you, Lord Jesus Christ"—

but it's nothing personal. We have a Bible and can read God's Word, but there's nothing personal there. Why? Because so many of us just go through the motions. The whole plan of God is to bring us into personal relationship, but for so many of us, it's nothing personal.

> THE WHOLE PLAN OF GOD IS TO BRING US INTO PERSONAL RELATIONSHIP, BUT FOR SO MANY OF US, IT'S "NOTHING PERSONAL."

So how can we take all that we encounter at church—from candles and robes to the Bible and the Mass—and make it personal? How can we move away from this feeling that Mass is "nothing personal" and toward having the Mass speak right to our hearts?

COMMUNICATING

We know in our friendships and our family relationships—and especially in dating and marriage—that communication is key. To get to know someone and to stay connected, we need to talk, and we need to listen.

The same is true for our relationship with God. If we want a personal relationship with God, we need to talk to God, and we need to listen to him. And that means we need to pray. Indeed, the only way to have a personal relationship with God is to pray.

So how do we pray?

"How do we pray?" is a big question. Many of us might respond, "I mean, I can *say* my prayers, but that's it. I don't really know how to *pray* pray, you know?" In fact, one of my buddies summed it up perfectly. He said as Catholics, we aren't taught how to pray, but rather how to repeat. For example, "Say after me: Our Father ..." And when we learn this way, we come to view prayer as a technique—one that some people are just better at than others. We think some people know how to do it, and other people don't.

But remember back in elementary school when you had to learn handwriting? You were probably either one of two kids: the one with perfect handwriting in kindergarten—who just got it and wrote letters perfectly—or the one who was jealous of that person. Honestly, I remember the girl in my class with perfect handwriting. She grew up and went to a great college, graduated early, and is a professor now. She was a genius, even as a child, and her handwriting was perfect. I would look over from my little sheet tracing letters, and she was already automatically so good at it. And in comparing my letter to hers, I came to this conclusion: "Well, I can't do it like that, so I guess I'm just not someone with good handwriting."

And that's what a lot of us do with prayer. We think it's a technique, like handwriting. And so we look at that person who's praying who looks totally into it—she's reading her Bible and crying, or he's in Adoration writing pages of notes in his journal—and think, "I don't pray like they do. I can't do it. I don't have the technique down."

If prayer was just a technique, like handwriting, that would mean that some people are going to be better at it than others. But think about the point of handwriting: The point of learning to write your letters is so that you can then communicate. It's not so you can just write perfect letters and have perfect technique.

Here's the thing: Prayer is not a technique. It's not about saying the right words. It's about communicating, and it's personal.

STEP ONE

I'm going to break down prayer into two simple steps.

Step one is that God loves you. No, really. Truthfully, step one when it comes to prayer, when it comes to taking it personally, has nothing to do with you doing anything. Step one is that God just loves you.

Remember when Jesus was teaching his disciples how to pray? He said this: "In praying, do not babble like the pagans, who think that they will be heard because of their many words. Do not be like them" (Matthew 6:7-8, NAB). And so let's press pause on the Scripture quickly and think about what Jesus meant there. How did the pagans pray? Who were the pagans? They were Romans and Greeks and Babylonians, those people in the ancient Middle East. What was their vision of the gods?

Pagan Gods

When I was a kid, I loved reading the Greek and Roman myths about Heracles or Hercules, Ares or Mars, and Aphrodite, Apollo, and Zeus. I thought they were super cool. But when you read these myths, you get to know a little bit about these gods. If you were a pagan, these were the kinds of gods you would pray to. So what were they like? They were radically different from the God Jesus reveals.

First, the gods of the pagans were not good. They were fickle, mean, cruel, selfish, angry, hostile, and crazy. So if you were a Roman, Greek, or Babylonian, you did not want the gods to pay attention to you because they were not good, and they didn't care about you. Even more, it would be ridiculous to think that any of the gods loved you.

Now, if you ever needed something from one of these gods, then you had to go to the temple because that's where they lived. Once there, you would first need to get the god's attention, and then you would need to earn their favor. But remember, the god was not paying attention to you because the god couldn't care less, wasn't good, and didn't love you. So you would have to be like, "Hey! Over here! Look at me, god! Now, give me this thing I want." You would go in and you'd offer an animal sacrifice to a particular god. And if you *were* able to get their attention and favor, the last step would be getting them to forget about you again!

If you were a Babylonian soldier going in to battle, for example, you would offer an animal sacrifice to the god of war. But if you really wanted to win the battle, then you would go a step further to make sure you gained their attention and favor. After the animal sacrifice, you would take out a dagger and start cutting yourself. You'd make it so that your blood would flow, and the idea was this: if you cut yourself and bled for this god, maybe he would pay attention to you. Maybe he'd give you what you want.

The God of Love

What you need to do is realize step number one: God already loves you. God is not like the pagan gods who don't care. You already have his attention. You already have his favor. He already cares about you. That's why Jesus says not to babble like the pagans when you pray.

I know some right now are thinking, "Well, yeah, but Christians do it anyways. We want to get God to pay attention to us. We come to Mass because we want to get God to give us stuff." My answer to that is, "Yes, we do, but that doesn't mean it makes sense." Honestly, how many times did Jesus have to let it be known that this isn't the way to pray? How much clearer did Jesus have to be when he told us to stop babbling like the pagans and thinking that our many words will get God's attention? Jesus tells us how to pray: just simply say "Our Father," and your Father who sees you and sees everything in secret, your Father who hears you and loves you, will answer you.

> YOUR FATHER WHO SEES YOU AND SEES EVERYTHING IN SECRET, YOUR FATHER WHO HEARS YOU AND LOVES YOU, WILL ANSWER YOU.

Think about when Jesus goes out into the wilderness for forty days. After being baptized by John in the Jordan, Jesus is led by the Holy Spirit into the wilderness. Let's take a look at what that means. In the time of the Old Testament, when someone was anointed king, it wasn't so that he could sit back and be fed grapes and be fanned with a palm frond; he was commissioned and consecrated to do one thing specifically: to go fight for his people. So look at Jesus. He gets baptized, and then the Holy Spirit comes upon him, anoints him, and then leads him into the wilderness where he battles the devil.

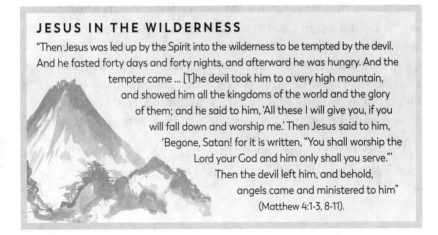

JESUS IN THE WILDERNESS

"Then Jesus was led up by the Spirit into the wilderness to be tempted by the devil. And he fasted forty days and forty nights, and afterward he was hungry. And the tempter came ... [T]he devil took him to a very high mountain, and showed him all the kingdoms of the world and the glory of them; and he said to him, 'All these I will give you, if you will fall down and worship me.' Then Jesus said to him, 'Begone, Satan! for it is written, "You shall worship the Lord your God and him only shall you serve."' Then the devil left him, and behold, angels came and ministered to him" (Matthew 4:1-3, 8-11).

Why does Jesus do it? Not for his health. Jesus does not go into the desert to fight Satan for his own benefit. He goes into the wilderness to fight Satan for you. If we think that we have to fight to get God's attention, if we think that we have to clamor or put on a show or bleed to get God to love us, think about where Jesus goes from here. What's at the end of these 40 days? Three years of ministry and then the Cross. For the Babylonian god of war, you had to bleed to get his attention. But the Christian God of love sheds his own blood to get your attention. He is willing to be cut to the heart to get your heart.

> ## JESUS GOES INTO THE WILDERNESS TO FIGHT SATAN FOR YOU.

In the book of Deuteronomy, Moses says how God's people were in a terrible situation, and just simply had to call out to the Lord, and he answered them (see Deuteronomy 26:6-9). Why does God answer? Because he loves us.

So this first step of taking it personally, the first step of prayer, is to realize that God loves us. He's watching. Now, that doesn't mean he's just watching what we're doing down here, hoping we're not messing up. People feel weird when you say "God is watching you," so a better way to say it is, "God is attentive to you." But that needs a clarification, too. When I say attentive, that doesn't mean God is your cosmic butler, doing every little thing you don't feel like doing. No, God is attentive to you, and that means he knows you and he's paying attention to you.

He's just waiting for you to look back at him. Why? Because God loves you. He loves you first. That's step one.

STEP TWO

But what does God want from me? That's step two: God wants you to let him love you. This sums up the Christian life—this is holiness in two steps; this is how to become a saint in two moves. One: God loves you. Two: you let him love you. That's it.

> STEP ONE: GOD LOVES YOU.
> STEP TWO: YOU LET HIM LOVE YOU.

Our problem with letting God love us is this—instead of letting God love us, we do one of three things. We dismiss his love, we disqualify ourselves from receiving it, or we say we earned it.

First, God says, "I love you; I love you first," and we put him in the friend zone. You probably know all about the friend zone, but here's what I mean by that. Maybe there's a young man and a young woman, and one of them says to the other, "I know we're great friends and I want you to know that I want to be more than friends." The person who says that is telling his friend that he doesn't just like her, he wants to enter into a relationship that could lead to marriage. If she's going to put him in the friend zone, what does she do? Typically, she doesn't address it straightforwardly—she doesn't say, "That's fantastic. I acknowledge that you care about me deeply, but I do not feel the same way. Let's go our separate ways." Typically, she reacts more like, "I'm just going to pretend you didn't say that. Let's just watch some more Netflix." That's typically what happens when we put someone in the friend zone. We don't talk directly to the other person about what he or she shared with us; we just ignore what that person said.

So one of the things we tend to do with God is this. We encounter the two steps of holiness—God loves you, you let him love you—and we say, "Oh, that's nice. I'll see you next Sunday." We don't let God love us; we just ignore the fact that he wants to take it to the next level. We just dismiss it.

The second thing we do is disqualify ourselves. We do that by saying three words: "Yeah, *but* I." God loves you—"Yeah, but I don't deserve that." God loves you first—"Yeah, but I mess up a ton." God loves you—"Yeah, but I've tried to pray and I just stink at it." God loves you—"Yeah, but I don't take it personally."

Saying "Yeah, but I" is all about disqualifying ourselves. I know so many of us are tempted to disqualify ourselves. God loves you—"Yeah, but I had a bad day yesterday and the last Saturday and Friday and Thursday and Wednesday. Father, this was a bad week." We either dismiss that God loves us or we disqualify ourselves from being near the God who loves us. We say, "Yeah, but I."

Now, there's a third thing we can do. This is what I did for years. In my first year of seminary, I went on a thirty-day silent retreat. It was basically thirty days just with Jesus. It was intimidating. The first half of the first day of the thirty-day retreat was supposed to be a meditation on God's love for you. I thought, "Piece of cake. I've got this down. I know God loves me; check. I'll let him love me; check." But when that meditation on God's love was supposed to finish, the retreat master said, "No, keep praying about God's love." Great. The next day, I checked in, and he said, "Keep going another day." Meditating on God's love was supposed to be just part of one day, but the retreat master kept me meditating on God's love for a week because he saw I was doing something that was a problem. I wasn't dismissing God's love, I wasn't disqualifying myself, but my thing was this: God loves you—"Yeah, *because* I." That was my trap: "Yeah, because I."

God loves you—"Yeah, because I'm a seminarian." God loves you—"Yeah, because I've been praying a lot." God loves you —"Yeah, because I've tried to be good." God loves you —"Yeah, because I'm a good guy." All these kinds of things kept coming up, and the retreat master kept hammering them away again and again. I was basically saying, "I've earned it." I was saying that somehow God loves me on a conditional basis. He loves me because I am a good person. But I had to stop because the reality is this: It's not "Yeah, because I"—it's "Yeah, because *he*."

He loves us because of who he is.

> GOD LOVES US BECAUSE OF WHO HE IS.

You may be struggling today with step two of prayer in one of those three ways: friend zoning God, disqualifying him with "yeah, but I," or thinking like I did for years that you earned it: "Yeah, because I." What we all need to hear is, "No, he loves you because he loves you. It's because of him."

HOW TO TAKE IT PERSONALLY

So when we go into prayer, these two steps have to be present. The first step is always God saying, "I love you." He loves you first. Before you do anything, he loves you first. The response we need to give is, "OK, Lord, I let you love me."

I'd like to propose an assignment for this week. If we're going to take prayer personally, we need to put these two steps into practice. Again, we're tempted to say, "No, it's nothing personal—this whole covenant thing, this whole Christianity thing, is nothing personal." But it actually is personal, and so we need to go to prayer and recognize that God loves us, and to let him love us.

People ask me, though, how do you do that? Because it seems like a technique still. Does it mean that we need to make it so we feel like God loves us or make it feel like he's present?

Think about Jesus in the wilderness. Do you think that Jesus felt like the Father was present with him there? He knew he was present, but he probably didn't feel it. And so we're not looking for a feeling. What we have to do is not to make it so we feel God's love—rather, it is to surrender to this truth. You just need to surrender. Just give up disqualifying yourself, give up dismissing yourself, or give up trying to validate yourself.

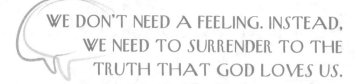

WE DON'T NEED A FEELING. INSTEAD, WE NEED TO SURRENDER TO THE TRUTH THAT GOD LOVES US.

There's this thirty-second video I came across of a little girl who's doing her homework. She's working on her handwriting, and she has to trace her letters. She is just sobbing. All this girl has to do is write a few more letters, but she's like, "I'm so tired." She's bawling her eyes out. Her mom is standing next to her, and her mom's like, "You can do it, it's OK." The little girl now only has three more letters to write, but she's sobbing, "But I'm so tired! I'll never be done by tonight." And her mom is reassuring her: "It's OK, just go ahead and write it."

If we think prayer is nothing personal, if we think it's just a technique, we make it so hard for ourselves. We go to prayer and think, *I'm so tired.* Why do we do this? Because we're trying to do this technique. We're trying to capture a feeling. We're trying to "accomplish" something. We're trying to perform or trying to prove something.

I watch that video, honestly, and I tear up. It's supposed to be funny, but when I see this little girl, I see so many people that I know. They think that prayer is nothing personal because they think that God doesn't really care. They think that it's just a technique because of how they see God. They think that God kind of is disgusted with them. When it comes down to it, they think that he doesn't really care if he gets to spend eternity with them or not. So many Catholics come to Mass and they're like, "Well, my vision of God is he doesn't really ultimately care. In fact, he would kind of rather spend eternity without me than with me."

But how much more does God have to do to demonstrate to you absolutely and fully that this whole thing, all of it, is so that you take it personally? It is all so that he can get to spend the rest of eternity with you. God loves you, *likes* you even.

When we go to prayer, God is standing next to us saying, "It's OK, just write your letters." Just pray. The point is not to have perfect letters. The point is not to have perfect prayer technique. If you know your letters, you can write a letter. The point of getting to know your alphabet is that you can then communicate. It doesn't matter if your handwriting is awful or awesome. And in prayer, you don't have to accomplish or achieve; you just have to surrender. Step one: God loves you already. Step two: just let him love you.

WATCH JESUS

Today, I invite you to do this: read the Gospel where Jesus goes into the wilderness. Your Bible is not meant to be a paperweight for your papers. It's there so you can do something with it. So I invite you to take some time to pick up the Gospel, Matthew 4, and read through it. Jesus is going into the wilderness—just watch him. That's it. As you read it, just watch. Watch him be led by the Holy Spirit. Just kind of sit and even go with him in your mind and say, "OK, Holy Spirit. Help me."

Watch Jesus as he goes in the desert. Walk next to him as he's being led. What does he look like as he's being led into the wilderness? Is he doing it with eagerness? Is he doing it with this glint in his eye, kind of like he's going to war as he battles Satan? Does he look over at you and give you a wink, like he's saying, "Doing this for you"? Does he have this hunger? This look of pain and sadness and sorrow and grief? Does he look like, "I could go another forty days because I'm doing this for you"? What does Jesus look like? Just watch him.

Read this Scripture today, watch Jesus, and then just think about it. It's not a technique, because it looks different for everybody. Watch him as he goes into the wilderness and fights for you because he loves you. Let him do that. Watch him fight for you and let him fight for you. That's the secret for holiness today. It's not a bunch of steps. Seeking holiness takes only two steps: God loves you; let him love you.

God wants to give you his mercy today. Let him. God has taken you and your wounds personally—so *let* him take you and your wounds personally.

REFLECT

Have you ever had an experience where bad communication created a difficult situation? What are some tips for good communication?

How is your communication with God? Are you using those tips for good communication with him? Are you disposing yourself to be able to have good conversations with him?

In the past, has it seemed like prayer is a technique that you can be good or bad at? Why is it important to know that prayer is about communication, not technique?

Has it ever felt like you had to earn God's attention before? If so, how does knowing that God is always listening change your perspective?

Did these two steps to prayer surprise you?

Do you have a personal relationship with God? If yes, please say something about that (for example, when did that start? How did it start?). If you don't, why do you think that that is?

Which of God's characteristics, revealed by Jesus, is the most important to you personally? (This question is more about you than about some kind of "theological importance.") For example, "Knowing this about God has changed my life." What is this?

Is it hard to believe that God simply loves you? Is it easier to believe that you have to still do more to get his attention or to make him love you more? Where do you think that comes from? If it is easy for you, why do you think that it is easy for you?

We can have a tendency to "dismiss" God's love, "disqualify" ourselves from his love, or believe that we "deserve" God's love. If you fall into any of these categories, what do you think is the best way out?

ACT

Read Matthew 4 in the ways described and reflect on how Jesus is fighting for you.

Chapter 2

FAITH AND FAITHFULNESS

I remember hearing about this study on generosity at a college campus where they went to the students in the dorms and were like, "OK, you've been living with these people. You've been eating with them, hanging out with them, studying with them—you know these people. Who is the most kind person in your dorm?" And so they collected a list of people that the students voted were the most kind, the most generous, the most shirt-off-your back type people in the dorm. But they also asked the students who was the least kind person in their dorm. Now, if you've lived in a dorm, you know the most kind person is pretty obvious. But the least kind person? They're usually even more obvious.

The college then sent each of these most and least kind students a letter indicating that they were going to do a food drive. It said, "We want to give people food, because it's really important to give people food. Anytime this week, go to the central plaza and drop some kind of canned food into the food drive bin."

By the end of the week, zero percent of the least kind students had given anything away. You'd kind of expect this; I mean, they're the least kind people. But of the people who were voted most kind, only eight percent had given anything to this food drive. Think about this. Of the most kind people in the dorms, only eight percent of them were willing to give food. My guess is that a hundred percent of them wanted to, but as humans we have a problem. We can know that we need to do something, we can even know that we want to do something, but we just don't do it.

THE PROBLEM

The same is true when it comes to prayer. I'm going to assume some things. I'm going to assume that if you're reading this, that you care about God. You either have met Jesus or you want to meet Jesus. I'm going to assume that at some level, more or less, you know that God has a plan for your life, and you actually want to act in a way that fits with that plan for your life.

Even further, I'll assume this: that you know God has made you to be a saint. Think about this: every saint who ever lived prayed. They're all different and they all have different personalities, they are from different parts of the world and they did different work, but every single one of them was united in that all of them prayed. Since you were made to be saint, you know that you need to pray.

So my guess, my assumption, is going to be this: not only that you know you need to pray—it's not optional—but you actually even *want* to pray. But we have a problem, because my other assumption is that not all of us are praying like we should.

PERSONAL RELATIONSHIP

If I were to ask you, "Is your prayer life like you want it to be?" my guess is your answer would be, "No. I wish I could pray more." We recognize that we don't have a prayer life, and yet the only way to have a personal relationship with God is to pray. And as I mentioned before, many Catholics are not convinced that you can even have a personal relationship with God. I'm assuming that you care about God and you want to pray, but for so many of us, it's nothing personal.

We come to Mass every single Sunday, some of us almost every day, to celebrate and to commemorate the fact that Jesus made it possible for us to have a relationship with God. And yet many of us don't think it's possible. That means that potentially half of the people reading these pages don't believe that it's even possible to have a personal relationship with God. Think about it in those terms.

How can we take it personally? How can we have that relationship God wants to have with us?

The only way to have a personal relationship with God is to pray, but like one of my buddies says, we as Catholics often aren't taught how to pray, we are taught how to repeat. We talked about this. It's as if we were taught how to write letters but we weren't taught how to put those together to make sentences or to communicate. That's why we need to recognize that prayer is not a technique. A technique is to say the right words, but prayer is not about a technique.

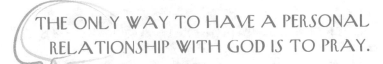

THE ONLY WAY TO HAVE A PERSONAL RELATIONSHIP WITH GOD IS TO PRAY.

FAITH

In the first chapter, we talked about the two steps of prayer: knowing God loves you already and letting him love you.

Here we'll talk about another lesson, which also has two steps. The first step of this lesson is to know God is present. That's the first step if you really want to pray, if you really want to make this something that's not impersonal but that is completely personal. We need to be absolutely convinced, absolutely committed to the truth that whenever we pray, God is there. The first step is called faith—commitment to the truth that God is present.

> ## THE FIRST STEP OF TAKING PRAYER PERSONALLY IS HAVING FAITH— HAVING COMMITMENT TO THE TRUTH THAT GOD IS PRESENT.

The reason you need faith is because, if you're like me, you'll go to prayer sometimes and not sense God being here. That's why we need to be committed to the truth that God is present. Faith.

We can think about this by looking at the Gospel of the Transfiguration. Here, Jesus takes Peter, James, and John up a high mountain, Mount Tabor. By this point, they've been walking with Jesus for years. That means they've been walking in God's presence. But on this mountain, Jesus gets transfigured, and they know they are in God's presence. His glory is revealed at that moment.

THE TRANSFIGURATION   "Jesus took with him Peter and James and John his brother, and led them up a high mountain apart. And he was transfigured before them, and his face shone like the sun, and his garments became white as light ... [A] bright cloud overshadowed them, and a voice from the cloud said, 'This is my beloved Son, with whom I am well pleased; listen to him'" (Matthew 17:1-2, 5).

Peter, James, and John were given this incredible faith. Why? Because Jesus revealed his glory and they knew that God was present. So even when they couldn't see his glory anymore, they knew he was still God. The Transfiguration only lasts a little while. Then Jesus makes them go down the mountain again, and they can't see his glory anymore. I keep imagining that Peter or James or John, who saw Jesus's glory, would be like, "Turn it back on." I imagine they probably wanted a button to turn on this transfiguration thing again. Why? Because in that moment, they could feel God's presence.

I imagine all of us probably want a button to turn on God's glory because we want to be able to feel God's presence. I want to be able to see God. I want to be able to have that faith that knows that God is present. But experiencing the Transfiguration was a gift for Peter, James, and John. It was just a gift to them. They didn't do anything to deserve it; they didn't do anything to earn it. Jesus just revealed it to them. It was a moment of grace.

God gives every one of us the grace we need. But it probably won't be like what Peter, James, and John had. We know that there were many other apostles and disciples who weren't on the mountain at that time. The other apostles and disciples didn't see the Transfiguration, but they had faith that God was present with them, too. They had that conviction and commitment to the truth of God's presence. They all prayed.

So your experience of God being present doesn't have to be the same as Peter, James, and John's experience, and it probably won't be. But we have to be committed to this truth. If we're going to pray, we need to have that conviction when we pray that God is there.

FAITHFULNESS

Step one of taking prayer personally is knowing God is present. The second step is being present yourself. Step one: we have faith that God is present. Step two: we have faithfulness, and we show up ourselves.

You know how the story goes, right? The same trio, that same Peter, James, and John who saw the Transfiguration, also go to the garden of Gethsemane. Jesus takes them off by themselves again there and says, "Remain here, and watch with me" (Matthew 26:38). He tells them to watch and pray with him. Stay awake. Be with him. What Peter, James, and John were given by Jesus on Mount Tabor was faith. But Gethsemane was where their faithfulness was meant to be forged.

Why do we show up? Why should we be present to Jesus in prayer? Because we get something out of it? Because he heals us? Because he lifts us up? All those things are good reasons— but the number one reason why we're called to faithfulness is because he asked us to be present. For Peter, James, and John in the garden, what are they getting out of this? Nothing. Why are they there? Because Jesus said, "Stay with me. Watch with me. Pray with me. Be here."

> WE'RE CALLED TO FAITHFULNESS BECAUSE GOD ASKS US TO BE PRESENT.

Why be faithful to prayer? Not because you're getting something. We don't get something out of every prayer. If we made it a requirement for ourselves that we needed to get something out of every prayer, then we probably wouldn't show up. We pray because Jesus asks us to pray. So his presence and our presence have to meet. Our faith that he is there and our faithfulness to being there, too, have to meet.

Think about Abraham, who was called Abram before God changed his name. Faith and faithfulness are Abram's story. In Genesis chapter 15, God says to Abram, "Look toward heaven, and number the stars, if you are able to number them" (Genesis 15:5). God tells Abram to see if he can count the stars, and he says that's how many descendants he's going to give Abram.

I don't know if you ever caught this detail about Abram's faith here. A few verses later, it says that "the sun was going down" (Genesis 15:12). So when God told Abram to look up into the sky and to see if he could count the stars if he could, he asked him to look up into the sky in the middle of the day. That's faith— believing that God is present even when you cannot see it.

Then Genesis chapter 15 says that God told Abram to cut up animals and make an aisle there for him. And then Abram sat down and deep, terrifying darkness came upon him. Abram stayed there. That's Abram's faithfulness.

So Abram has faith that God is present, and then Abram responds with faithfulness. He is present. This is the mark of Abram's life. All of Abram's life is focused on faith and faithfulness. God is present, and Abram is present. His whole life becomes this process of becoming the person he's called to be. Why? Because of faith and faithfulness.

CONSISTENCY BEATS INTENSITY

Faith and faithfulness are part of a process, but so often I don't want it to be a process. I want to be able to experience this intense encounter with God and be like, "OK, now I'm good and I know I'm holy." I want it to be over with. But God shows us that this has to be a process. Why? Because a process implies time.

Think about what faithfulness is, if not love extended through time. Faithfulness, showing up, is love extended through time.

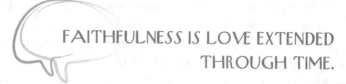

FAITHFULNESS IS LOVE EXTENDED
THROUGH TIME.

We know this is true when it comes to our personal relationships. Almost all of our personal relationships have to have faithfulness over time. We realize there's no such thing as true love if there's no such thing as faithfulness. That's why a person who cannot be faithful is incapable of love.

Part of love is being able to say, "I promise you that I'll show up," and then to keep showing up. Believing that the other person will be present is faith, and showing up myself is faithfulness. But if I promise to be there when I really can't promise to be there—I'm unable to love.

Of course, when it comes to relationships and romance, we want intensity. When Valentine's Day comes around, we want to shower the other person or to be showered with all these incredible gifts. But the day after Valentine's Day, we would not be happy to hear, "OK, sweet. Wasn't that pretty good? I'm going to ignore you now."

We realize this in our relationships: consistency beats intensity every time.

Let's illustrate this with a story. A couple has been dating for some time and have fallen in love. The guy says to his girlfriend: "I'm going to surprise you with a trip this weekend. Just have a bag packed. In that bag, pack a nice dinner outfit and then whatever else you need for the weekend, and be at your home at four o'clock on Friday."

So she packs her things, the doorbell rings at four o'clock, and she goes downstairs to find a limo waiting for her. In the back of the limo there's a little envelope that reads, "You're going to the airport. Here's a plane ticket to New York City." She gets to the airport and flies first class to New York City, where another limo awaits her. And there's another envelope on the seat that reads, "You're going to this hotel. Here's your room key." She goes to the hotel, and her room is the top penthouse decorated with flowers and candles. There she finds another card that says, "You're signed up for a day at the spa. Just come to the lobby at six o'clock." That evening, she goes to the lobby, where another limo and another envelope await her, and the driver drops her off at the Empire State Building. She goes to the top of this impressive building like the card told her to do. And there she sees her boyfriend, down on one knee with a ring and a proposal.

If you're like me, you hear this story and think, "Wait, dude! You just shot yourself in the foot! What are you going to do for your first anniversary to top that?!"

Seriously, of course, that's a huge moment of intensity, an incredibly intense romantic gesture. But while that might be an incredible weekend and proposal, I guarantee you that every one of us would rather have someone who is consistently faithful to us than someone who is randomly intense with us. All of us know this: consistency beats intensity every single time.

FAITHFULNESS TO A PERSON

Consistency beats intensity when it comes to our relationship with God, as well. I say that I want to have this mountaintop experience on Mount Tabor, or this intense experience of wanting to stay up here praying for days, and God says, "No. Just show up for fifteen minutes per day for the rest of your life." God wants consistency, not intensity. God wants faithfulness, not just a one-shot thing.

The reality is that prayer is about a person. When we go to prayer, this is not just a task. It's not just a discipline. It's not just saying, "OK, I said I'd do this, so here I am." It's fidelity or faithfulness to a person.

> ## FAITHFULNESS TO PRAYER IS FAITHFULNESS TO A PERSON.

We're tempted to think it's nothing personal. But if you write down a time when you're committed to pray and you don't show up, you're denying Jesus, a person. It's completely personal. If you skip it, you're saying no to someone. If you show up, you're saying yes to someone. Faithfulness is saying, "I will be there."

PLAN IT OUT

We're called to be saints, and we can't become saints unless we pray. The most important thing you can do with your day is to talk to God, because it's something incredibly personal. So how can we overcome the problem of knowing we need to do it and yet not doing it? How do we respond with faithfulness?

We need to plan it out.

Here's what I invite you to do. Don't just think, *I'm going to pray more this week*. Instead, I ask you to do this: give God fifteen minutes this week, every day. I heard a priest say once that five minutes is the amount of time we give to someone when we're trying to get rid of that person politely. That's true. So don't give God five minutes, give him fifteen minutes every day. And during those fifteen minutes, here's what I want you to do. Look up the Gospel every day and pray with it, read it.

Before the week starts, write down when those fifteen minutes are going to happen. When are you going to talk to Jesus? When are you going to watch him in the Gospels? Write this down.

I know where I'm going to go to pray because we have a chapel in my house, so I don't have to decide where I should go. But I want you to write down where you're going to be to pray.

Tonight, before you go to bed, please write down when and where you are going to spend those fifteen minutes with God. That is something incredibly personal, to be able to look at God and say, "God, here it is. I will be there."

When it all comes down to it, we get one life. The most important thing we can do with that life is to have a relationship with God. I know that you know you need to, and I know that you want to. Let's come to prayer with faith and faithfulness. Let's make a plan and stick to it, and let's pray not just when we feel it, but when we don't as well. God is waiting for you.

REFLECT

If you could go back to kindergarten, what is one thing that you wish you had started practicing and stuck with (so that you would be an expert in it now)? For example, "I wish I had started learning Cantonese/the violin/gymnastics/yodeling ..."

Is your prayer life how you want it to be?

Do you think it's possible to have a relationship with God?

Have you ever *felt God's presence during prayer? If so, what was that experience like? Why do you think it's important for us to have moments when we don't feel his presence, as well as moments when we do?*

Is it hard *to know that God is present to us?*

Sometimes, it is difficult *for us to be present in prayer. What are some difficulties you have experienced being present in prayer, and what are some good ways to overcome them?*

Do you agree *that consistency beats intensity every single time? And why is this true in prayer especially?*

Have you ever *thought about how faithfulness in prayer is faithfulness to a person? How can this change the way we look at consistency in prayer?*

Have you ever *made a plan for your prayer before? If so, how did it go?*

We will never be saints unless we pray. *But we experience obstacles. What is the single most difficult obstacle that you encounter in your commitment to be consistent to daily prayer?*

ACT

Make a plan *for your daily fifteen minutes of prayer this week. Write down when and where you're going to spend time in conversation with God.*

Chapter 3

FEAR AND FEARLESSNESS

I recently came across a video of a man who was live tweeting his wedding—his own wedding—as it was happening. Another video clip I saw was of this man who stopped the minister as soon as he and his bride had said their vows, pulled out his phone, and updated his Facebook status from engaged to married. It kind of reminds me of a video of this couple that came down the wedding aisle to Chris Brown's "Forever," which was also a scene in *The Office*. I remember watching it thinking, "That's really funny, but at the same time ... huh." Because for the folks in those videos, it seems to be the apex of their wedding to see how entertaining or, in a certain way, how silly they can be.

SOMETHING SACRED

I want to compare that and contrast it to a wedding Mass I just celebrated recently. I'll call the groom Charlie and the bride Jamie. This couple approached the wedding in a different way—like it was something sacred. And so a half hour before the wedding, Charlie got all of his groomsmen in a room by themselves and said, "OK, guys, we're going to pray the Rosary together, because we're going to get ready for this." And Jamie got all of her bridesmaids together and said, "OK, we're going to pray the Rosary together. We're going to get ready for this."

It wasn't entertainment—no, this was a holy thing. This was a sacred thing. And so at two o'clock we're all ready; I'm back in the sacristy with Charlie, a deacon, and a server, and the deacon says, "It's time to go out." So we walk out, and then we stand there. Everyone's looking at us, but the musicians are up in the loft just chatting and strolling around. We're standing there right in the front, waiting for the music to begin, and one minute goes by and another minute goes by, and the musicians are just completely unaware that we're there. Seriously for three minutes we just stood there. I was wishing I had Jedi mind powers to communicate to the musicians to start. Finally, the musicians looked down and saw us, like, "Oh, there's a priest and there's the guy in the tux." They looked at Charlie and looked at their watches and Charlie said, "Yep, right now." Everyone laughed, and the musicians were like, "I thought we were starting at 2:30." And Charlie said, "Nope, two o'clock."

It was one of those moments that broke the ice. It was a moment of laughter, but it was more than just laughter. It was not a moment of silliness. I don't want to be too spiritual about it, but it truly was a moment of holy joy. I know this because of what happened next.

As the groomsmen started walking down the aisle, Charlie did something unconventional. Charlie is a rule follower, but he stepped off the steps where the groom usually stands. As his brothers and his friends started walking down the aisle and got to the base of the steps, he gave each one a hug as if to say, "I'm so glad you're here."

Then he stepped back up, the door opened, and his bride started walking down the aisle toward him. This man was just overcome. He was absolutely overwhelmed. Tears were rolling down his cheeks, and it was clear that he realized something. This moment was not a silly moment; this moment was a holy moment. Because he realized that, he didn't just entertain his friends on Facebook or invite people to watch him dance down the aisle or do something silly. His attitude was, "I invite you here because I'm going to do something really dangerous. I'm going to do something that I've never done in my life. I need you here to witness this, and I need you to pray with me."

And that kind of sacred thing he was doing and his awareness that it was sacred enabled him to have both the moment of joy—laughing at "yeah, we're late"—and then also the overwhelmed moment.

I think we don't have enough overwhelmed moments in our lives. You might be way different than I am, but I think I sometimes tend to have more silly moments. I don't often get to experience a moment of just absolutely being overwhelmed by another person or even what we're going to talk about today—being overwhelmed by God.

OVERWHELMED BY GOD

You know we've been talking about the idea so many of us have about faith—the idea "it's nothing personal." So many of us don't have a personal relationship with God. We talked about coming to prayer—recognizing that God loves us and letting God love us, and believing that he is present and being present and faithful ourselves. Here we're going to talk about another part of a personal relationship with God.

So many of us have never been overwhelmed by God. We've never been aware that we are in God's presence, and this is serious. Why? Because most of us—not everyone, but most of us—grew up going to Mass. And so when it comes to the idea of approaching Holy Communion, when it comes to the idea of approaching Jesus in the Eucharist, we're like, "Yeah, I'm used to it." It's common. It's kind of ordinary. And there's not this sense of being overwhelmed.

The Bible talks of being overwhelmed in a very specific way. The Bible uses the term "fear of the Lord."

Think about the story of Moses. You probably know his backstory because we all saw *The Prince of Egypt*—Moses was raised in Egypt in the house of Pharaoh. Growing up in Pharaoh's house, Moses would have known about all these different gods the Egyptians worshipped.

After Moses grew up, he left Pharaoh's house because he had to flee into the desert. He lived in the desert for forty years. By that point, he was an old man, and he thought he knew something about life.

Exodus chapter 3 tells the story of what happens next: the story of the burning bush. Moses saw this bush that was burning but not being consumed. When he first saw it, it says in Scripture, he was surprised to see a bush that was burning but not consumed. I guess that's an adequate response, to be startled by the sight of the bush. Moses approaches the bush, and then he hears God speak to him from the bush. Moses even seems to be able to respond, until the moment when God says, "Take off your shoes." It's a holy moment. And God says, "I am the God of your fathers. I am the God of Abraham, Isaac, and Jacob."

THE BURNING BUSH

"He looked, and lo, the bush was burning, yet it was not consumed. And Moses said, 'I will turn aside and see this great sight, why the bush is not burnt.' When the LORD saw that he turned aside to see, God called to him out of the bush, 'Moses, Moses!' And he said, 'Here am I.' Then he said, 'Do not come near; put off your shoes from your feet, for the place on which you are standing is holy ground.' And he said, 'I am the God of your father, the God of Abraham, the God of Isaac, and the God of Jacob.' And Moses hid his face, for he was afraid to look at God." (Exodus 3:2-6).

Now, think back to Egypt. When Moses was in Egypt, there were a bunch of gods that he knew the Egyptians worshipped, but they were impersonal gods. There was a god of the sun, a god of the Nile, a god of frogs, a god of fleas, a god of cattle—and all of a sudden, at the burning bush, here is God who reveals, "I actually am a personal God, and I'm coming after you. I'm a personal God, and I'm pursuing you."

And the very next line is that Moses hid his face because he was terrified. Why was Moses afraid? Because this is not a god who's off in the sun. If he was in the sun, every night I could get to take a break from him. He's not a god who's at the Nile. If he was at the Nile, if I wanted, I could walk away from him. This is a God of relationships. This is a personal God, and I cannot hide from him. In fact, he's pursuing me.

> THIS IS A PERSONAL GOD, AND I CANNOT HIDE FROM HIM.

FEAR OF THE LORD

Moses experiences a profound fear in this encounter. The Bible talks about fear of the Lord all the time. To understand that, let's pause and ask a question. When you hear those words, what do you think?

I think in our day and age, we don't like the idea of fear of the Lord. I think that it makes us uncomfortable; we're kind of resistant to it. And yet, again, the Bible talks about it. In fact, the Bible says that if you don't have fear of the Lord, you cannot be wise—the beginning of wisdom is having the fear of the Lord. We even actually believe that one of the seven gifts of the Holy Spirit is fear of the Lord.

FEAR OF THE LORD

"The fear of the LORD is the beginning of wisdom" (Proverbs 9:10).

THE SEVEN GIFTS OF THE HOLY SPIRIT

"The seven *gifts* of the Holy Spirit are wisdom, understanding, counsel, fortitude, knowledge, piety, and fear of the Lord. They belong in their fullness to Christ, Son of David. They complete and perfect the virtues of those who receive them" (CCC 1831, original emphasis).

In fact, if we look at basically any time in the whole Bible when God approaches someone, that is their experience as they encounter the real God and they are able to let God be God. For example, Isaiah says, "Woe is me!" (Isaiah 6:5). Basically, he says, "I'm dead. Here comes God—he's coming after me, he's a personal God coming after me."

So what do we think of when we think of fear of the Lord? Is fear of the Lord the same as normal fears we have? This isn't true, but if you thought so, you're not the first person to think that. If we go all the way back to the three hundreds, there's this bishop named St. Hilary of Poitiers. He once said that when we think of fear of the Lord, "fear" is not to be taken in the same way that common usage gives it. He says fear in the ordinary sense is trepidation, what our weak humanity feels when we're afraid of suffering something that we don't want to happen. So I'm afraid of my child leaving the Church, I'm afraid of losing my job, I'm afraid of not graduating from school, I'm afraid of going into surgery, I'm afraid of whatever it is that I don't want to happen.[2]

Then St. Hilary goes on to say that we're also made afraid because of a guilty conscience or because of the rights of someone more powerful. We're afraid of an attack of one who's stronger, or we're afraid of sickness, or we're afraid of encountering a wild beast. (That happened back in the day.) We're afraid of suffering evil in any form. St. Hilary says that's not what we're talking about when we talk about fear of the Lord.

Because when it comes to fear of the Lord, what it ultimately boils down to is letting God be God. Fear of the Lord is this: I realize there's a God who is a person, or Trinity of persons, and he wants to be close to me. He is so good and he wants to be close to me.

IN AWE

I think many Catholics are told that God is great and good, but they stop there. We stop getting close to him. And so that's why we have this thing called Catholic guilt. Now, my mom, whenever she talks about Catholic guilt, always says, "What's so Catholic about guilt? Guilt isn't something Catholic. If you've done something wrong, you should feel guilty." But the idea behind Catholic guilt comes from not wanting to get close to God. When we were kids, we heard about this God out there who can see you when you're sleeping and knows when you're awake, and he knows when you've been bad or good so be good. I mean, I don't want a personal relationship with that kind of God. So most Catholics stop there. That's when they stop learning about God. That's when many people stop going to Mass. That's why we have this whole weird concept called Catholic guilt.

I want to say let's move past this. We need to have fear. It's the same kind of fear that's in the Bible. Even the angels are in awe before God.

> ## EVEN THE ANGELS ARE IN AWE BEFORE GOD.

Now, when you think angels, please don't think the little chubby babies, and don't think Tinkerbell flitting around. The angels in Scripture are these immensely powerful, beautiful, wise, incredible beings. The prophet Isaiah talks about the angels that come before God (see Isaiah 6:1-8). Just imagine the scene. Isaiah describes them as having six wings. One set of wings covers their feet. The idea behind that is they won't go anywhere unless God tells them to go. Their feet are at God's service. One set of wings they hold aloft, ready to move whenever God wants them to. But the amazing thing is that the final set of wings covers their faces in the presence of God. Think about this. The God that we're serving at every Mass, the God we're worshiping every day—angels cover their faces so they don't see him. They don't look upon him. This is why Moses falls to the ground and covers his face. He's afraid and says, "Don't come any closer."

This is the One that you will receive into your mouth in the Eucharist—and angels can't even look at him in the face.

THE FATHER WHO LOVES YOU

In trying to think of an image that can capture this, those YouTube videos of soldiers returning home came to mind. They're videos of fathers returning home to their families and surprising their kids—and the kids turn around and at that moment realizes their dad is here. They realize, "My father has now returned home. My father's in my presence now." And oftentimes what happens is they either fall to their knees or they cover their faces. Oftentimes, they're overcome. They're overwhelmed, and then they race to him.

In some sense, this captures what the real fear of the Lord is supposed to elicit in us. It's not meant to be a sense of "I can't stay. I have to be gone. I'm afraid of him." That would be a whole different story, wouldn't it? If there's a bad dad showing up, "daddy's home" would not be good. But that's not the God who pursues you. That's not the God who arrives. The God who arrives is the God who's a good dad. He is a good Father. He loves you.

That's why fear of the Lord goes with love of the Lord. In the Bible, in Deuteronomy 10, it talks about fear of the Lord, but it alternates between talking about fear and love. If you fear the Lord, you're going to love the Lord. And the more you love the Lord, the more you're going to fear the Lord. Because we realize this: that fear is the first stage of wisdom. But fear is not the last stage of wisdom. You know what the goal of wisdom is? Love.

FEAR OF THE LORD GOES WITH LOVE OF THE LORD.

St. John said, "Perfect love casts out fear" (1 John 4:18). We need to have fear of the Lord, but God wants us to have more. If we're going to have a personal relationship with the Lord, we also need fearlessness.

FEARLESSNESS

In fact, Psalm 112 says this: "Blessed is the man who fears the Lord, who greatly delights in his commandments" (Psalm 112:1). It goes on: "His heart is steady, he will not be afraid" (Psalm 112:8). You realize you've encountered God as God, and you'll never be shaken.

> "BLESSED IS THE MAN WHO FEARS THE LORD, WHO GREATLY DELIGHTS IN HIS COMMANDMENTS ... HIS HEART IS STEADY, HE WILL NOT BE AFRAID"
>
> (Psalm 112:1, 8).

And the psalmist says, "The righteous will never be moved ... He is not afraid of evil tidings" (Psalm 112:6-7). One who fears the Lord does not fear bad news. How many people watch a twenty-four-hour news network and are shaken with fear, wondering, "What's the next crisis of the age? What's the next thing that could go wrong?"

But the ones who fear the Lord are fearless. They do not fear what could go wrong. Their hearts are steadfast, trusting in the Lord. Their hearts are tranquil. They live their lives with fearlessness. Why? Because they have fear of the Lord. Therefore, they do not need to fear anything else—not even their weakness.

Too many of us realize that we are in the presence of the good God who pursues us and wants us, and we realize we don't belong in his presence, and then we stop. Instead of being able to approach God with fearlessness, we stop. If we allow God to be God, then not only do we not have to be afraid of what's going to happen with life, but we also do not even have to be afraid of our own sin. We don't even have to be afraid of our own weakness.

In Exodus 3, Moses sees God and hides his face. He's afraid. Later, Exodus chapter 33 says this: after a time, when Moses let God be God, then Moses would enter into the tent in the presence of God, and he would speak to God. Exodus says, "The LORD used to speak to Moses face to face, as a man speaks to his friend" (Exodus 33:11).

Being able to speak to God face to face was a special gift that God gave to Moses, but this fearlessness is meant to be yours, too. It's your inheritance. Do you realize that as Catholics, your inheritance is to be able to come into God's presence with fearlessness? But it's not a fearlessness that's based on your courage. It's not a fearlessness that's based on how good you are. It's not a fearlessness based on how you've organized your life. It doesn't mean you can approach God with confidence, courage, or fearlessness because you're pretty much as good as he is. That's false.

TRUST

True Christian fearlessness has nothing to do with bringing anything to God except your own weakness. So true fearlessness takes trust. It takes not trusting yourself, but rather trusting in God. Let's look at the example of St. Teresa of Ávila, an incredible woman from the sixteenth century. Teresa was a nun, and she talked about how she struggled with coming before God. She said that she had fear of the Lord. She realized he is awesome. He overwhelmed Teresa with his love. She was overwhelmed with God's goodness—but she realized she didn't love him back as she should. Therefore, she considered herself disqualified. She didn't think she could have real, deep prayer in his presence.

TRUE FEARLESSNESS TAKES TRUST IN GOD.

Teresa said she lived like that for a year and a half until she talked to this Dominican priest who told her she needed to go into God's presence with her weakness and give it to him. And then she could have fearlessness. So she stopped trying to impress God. She couldn't make herself great and give him her own greatness. And when she went into his presence with weakness, then God did amazing things in her life.[3]

There's another girl whose name was Thérèse, and she got her name from Teresa. Thérèse went into the convent at age fifteen and died at twenty-four. Though she lived a short life, Thérèse is an incredible example of someone who was fearless. On her deathbed, she was being suffocated by tuberculosis. It was making her lungs fill up, and she was hardly able to breathe. As she was lying there, this nun came in and did something that irritated Thérèse, and Thérèse snapped back at her. You can imagine that if you're suffocating because your lungs are filling up with fluid, you kind of have permission to have a bad day. But Thérèse was trying to be a saint.

Keep in mind that a year after Thérèse died, the convent started getting letters from all over the world. People were saying, "Thérèse interceded for me and I have a miracle." She's now one of the thirty-four doctors of the church—this girl is a mega saint. She's this serious, amazing saint at age twenty-four.

When Thérèse recognized she had snapped at her sister, she could have said, "Well, I don't even know why I'm doing this. I don't belong here. Why am I even trying to be a saint?" Instead, she was like, "Jesus, you know me. You know how weak I am. I'm so sorry. Look how funny I am. I'm about to see you face to face hours from now, and I just snapped at my sister. I'm so sorry. Please, Jesus, make up for my own weakness, because I can't do it on my own."[4]

THE GOODNESS OF GOD

If we want to have that fearlessness like St. Thérèse of Lisieux, if we want to have personal relationship, if we want it to be more than this impersonal thing, here's what we need to do: We need to let God be God.

> IF WE WANT TO HAVE FEARLESSNESS,
> WE NEED TO LET GOD BE GOD.

Here's what I mean. There's the parable about the prodigal son. We've all heard it, so I will just hit on the main points. There's a son, he goes to his father, and he says, "Father, give me my share of the inheritance." The dad gives it, and the son goes off. He wastes the whole thing. He gets hungry and he's about to die, so he decides to go back home. And before he starts back home, he works out this speech: "Father, I have sinned against heaven and before you; I am no longer worthy to be called your son; treat me as one of your hired servants" (Luke 15:18-19).

THE PRODIGAL SON "The younger son gathered all he had and took his journey into a far country, and there he squandered his property in loose living ... But when he came to himself he said, 'How many of my father's hired servants have bread enough and to spare, but I perish here with hunger! I will arise and go to my father, and I will say to him, "Father, I have sinned against heaven and before you; I am no longer worthy to be called your son; treat me as one of your hired servants." And he arose and came to his father. But while he was yet at a distance his father saw him and had compassion, and ran and embraced him and kissed him. And the son said to him, 'Father, I have sinned against heaven and before you; I am no longer worthy to be called your son.' But the father said to his servants, 'Bring quickly the best robe, and put it on him; and put a ring on his hand, and shoes on his feet ... for this my son was dead, and is alive again; he was lost, and is found.' And they began to make merry" (Luke 15:13, 17-22, 24).

So he has this whole thing rehearsed, but who's it all about? It's all about him. He's saying, "Father, I'm super bad. I'm terrible. I'm awful. Please treat me as one your hired workers." So he gets up and he goes to the father's home. When the father sees him a long way off, he races to his son and the son has the speech ready, right? He says, "Father, I have sinned against heaven and against you. I no longer deserve to be called your son." And the father stops him and begins rejoicing. You can imagine in that moment the son is like, "No, listen; I have this whole thing rehearsed." And the dad's like, "No, we're going to have a party." And the son's like, "No, Father, you don't know how bad I am." The father's like, "No, listen. We're going to give you my finest robe." The son's like, "Father, I'm an awful person." The father says, "No, we're going to slaughter the fattened calf for you." The son is like, "No, you don't get it. You don't know how bad I am." And the father has to stop and say, "Stop. No, you don't know how good *I* am."

So often we come before God as if we are saying, "God, you don't know how bad I am." And he stops us and says, "Stop. You don't know how good I am." This is not just the story of the prodigal son; this is the story of the generous father.

If we're going to have fearlessness, we have to stop thinking about ourselves so much. But we're a bunch of little narcissists, right? When we come to prayer, we're like, "God, I'm so bad. I'm so awful. I'm so whatever." Or we have on the other side, "I'm so awesome. I'm so amazing. I'm so incredible."

To be overwhelmed by God is to say, "God, I don't have anything to give, but you're so good. I'm going to stand here. Unless you put the robe on me, I don't have anything to offer. God, I'm going to stand here and let you put a ring on my finger. I'm going to stand here as long as you love me."

In one of those videos of soldiers coming home, there's this little girl whose dad walks in the room and she looks up and she can't move. She just stands there, and she starts to cry. She covers her face. And the dad goes over to her. He just wraps his arms around her, and he holds her to him.

LET GOD BE GOD

Sometimes, we're like that in prayer. We think, "I just can't do anything here. I have nothing to give. I have nothing to offer. I can't take a step toward you." We just stand there, overwhelmed by fear. It's time to let God be God, to let yourself be overwhelmed by his presence and his incredible power, but also to let God be God and be fearless and to let him take you in his arms. When we want to say, "I have nothing to give you," we need to let him say, "You don't have to give anything; just let me hold you."

That's why I invite you to do something today. Read Psalm 131. It's just three verses long. Psalm 131 says that God's marvels are beyond us. The psalmist says to the Lord that he hasn't gone after things too big. He's not great, but he's set his soul in silence and in peace like a child that rests in his mother's arms. We can pray that psalm and ask God to just hold us. Let God be God.

Let God be God. Experience the fear of the Lord so that you can experience fearlessness in the rest of your life, and in the presence of the Lord.

REFLECT

In the past, what have you thought "fear of the Lord" meant? How is this different from the way it was just described (see page 36, "Fear of the Lord")?

Have you ever felt like you had to make yourself great? Why is it so powerful that we can let God make us great?

Have you ever thought about the story of the prodigal son as also being the story of the generous father? If not, what do you think of this idea?

What is one thing that you used to be afraid of as a child? How did that start? Did you ever get over that fear? How?

Moses was merely "interested" in God's presence in the burning bush ... until God revealed himself as the God of relationship. Do you think people would prefer to have a God of relationships, or a god like the gods of Egypt (impersonal and restricted to locations and situation)?

St. Hilary of Poitiers makes it clear that "fear of the Lord" is not "fear" in the normal sense. Do you have a difficult time making the distinction between "being afraid of God" and "fear of the Lord"? Why might you think that this is the case?

Psalm 112 reveals that the person who fears the Lord fears nothing else. The saints testify that they do not even fear their own sin or weakness. Noting that this is not the same as "making light" of one's sins, what can make it difficult to trust in God's goodness this deeply?

In prayer, we all have a tendency to be a bit narcissistic (or "self-preoccupied"). We may tend to focus on our badness when God desires us to place our attention on him. Is this easy or difficult (or a non-issue) for you?

ACT

Continue with your daily prayer plan, and read Psalm 131.

Chapter 4

THE BATTLE OF PRAYER

If I told you my brother-in-law Tanner grew up on a goat ranch in Oklahoma (which is true), how might you picture him? You might imagine this tall lanky guy who always wears cowboy boots and kind of talks with a drawl and smells a lot like manure. That's what I would picture, and maybe that's similar to what you would picture.

But if you met Tanner, you would realize, OK, he's tall and lanky, I mean, at least as tall as I am, but he wears tennis shoes more often than not, he has no drawl whatsoever, and he smells pretty good.

So let's say you knew before meeting him that Tanner grew up on a goat ranch in Oklahoma. What happens when you meet him for the first time and see he doesn't fit that stereotype in your mind? You realize that what you knew about him isn't wrong, it just gets purified. And this is the case whenever we hear about someone and then get to know that person. If what you heard about someone was true, it doesn't change when you get to know the person, but it gets purified. It gets deeper.

In a certain sense, it gets truer. It gets more accurate to the person. And this has to happen with all of us when it comes to knowing Jesus.

KNOWING JESUS CHRIST

In St. Paul's letter to the Philippians, he says, "I count everything as loss because of the surpassing worth of knowing Christ Jesus" (Philippians 3:8). He is saying that he counts everything to be a loss compared with the supreme joy of knowing Jesus.

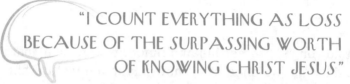

"I COUNT EVERYTHING AS LOSS BECAUSE OF THE SURPASSING WORTH OF KNOWING CHRIST JESUS"

(Philippians 3:8).

Now, I've been thinking about this a lot, this idea of knowing Jesus Christ. A lot of us who have been raised in the Church know *about* Jesus. But a lot of us don't *know* Jesus. Again and again I encounter people who struggle to know Jesus, especially people who went to Catholic school. Maybe you had to go to Mass every single Sunday; maybe you sat in a lot of Catholic school classes. If that's you, then right now, at this point in your life, you can say, "I know a ton about Jesus." But we have to realize there is a tremendous difference between knowing *about* Jesus and *knowing* Jesus.

Why is this important? Because we've been talking about this idea that "it's nothing personal." A lot of us as Catholics know about God, but very few of us would say, "I know God." So when we show up to Mass or we talk about God or we read about God, or even when we try to pray, it's nothing personal. We know about God, but we don't recognize that we come to

Mass and meet Jesus. We don't realize that we read the Bible and hear God's voice. When we go to pray, we don't experience that we're talking with a God we know. Few of us would say, "I know him."

But this difference between knowing about God and knowing God is so profound that St. Paul says, "For his sake I have suffered the loss of all things, and count them as refuse" (Philippians 3:8). I love this translation of "refuse." The word that St. Paul used for refuse is a Greek word for excrement. It's actually an earthy word. He used a swear word. This is a devotional book, so we clean it up. St. Paul says that he considers everything refuse compared to the supreme joy of knowing Jesus. He is filled with joy because he knows Jesus, he doesn't just know about him. Why would he say this? Because when we come to know Jesus, everything we know about him is purified, and it's all transformed. It is all new because we now have a personal relationship with a personal God that we now know. That knowledge about him had to be purified.

THE SEASON FOR CONTINUING

But here's the next step. If you've met him, if you've started this whole process of knowing Jesus and trying to have a personal relationship with him, the next step is not just purifying our knowledge of him. We have to purify our love. That's what I want to talk about here: the step of purifying our love. Because when we get to know Jesus, that has to happen. And here's what I mean.

TO HAVE A PERSONAL RELATIONSHIP WITH JESUS, WE DON'T JUST PURIFY OUR KNOWLEDGE OF HIM. WE HAVE TO PURIFY OUR LOVE.

On January 1st, if you're like the rest of humanity, you probably started something new. Maybe you made a resolution like, "I'm going to read more. I'm going to eat more healthy food. I'm going to exercise more." Probably you started something in the first week of January because New Year's Day is the season for starting. But the rest of the year after January is the season for continuing.

Think about Lent. The beginning of Lent is Ash Wednesday. That's the season for starting. Each year, all of us as Catholics start something on Ash Wednesday, like, "I'm going to pray more. I'm going to get closer to the Lord. I'm going to start fasting more." That is the season for starting—but as Lent goes on, that is the season for continuing.

The reason I want to point this out is because St. Paul says this: "I count everything as loss because of the surpassing worth of knowing Jesus Christ" (Philippians 3:8). But then he goes on to say, "Not that I have already obtained this or am already perfect; but I press on to make it my own, because Christ Jesus has made me his own" (Philippians 3:12). St. Paul continues. He can say, "I press on. I keep moving forward. I keep striving forward. I continue." This idea comes back again and again and again: I continue, I continue, I continue.

There was a season for starting, and there is a season for continuing. There's a personal God I can know personally. When I began to pray, that was when I started. But now it's the season for continuing. Now it's the season to get deeper. Now it's the season where relationships either thrive or die.

Recently I was talking to a college student. He met this girl on campus and was overwhelmingly infatuated with her. For over a year and a half, he's done the whole, "Hey, we're friends, or whatever, so let's study together." Some of you women reading this are probably thinking, "I know a guy like that or I knew a guy like that. I did not like that guy." That guy spends time with a girl and studies with her and all these kinds of things, but he leaves it there. They're friends.

This guy knew a lot about this girl. He told me recently, "I can't ask her out. I can't, because she's my dream girl." I'm like, "She's your dream girl, and therefore you won't ask her out? Dude, if you don't act soon, she'll be gone." And he said, "Well, I know. But if I act and she says no, then I'm done." I'm like, "You're a coward. You're a scaredy cat," because he didn't want to say something or try to start a relationship and get shot down. (Any single men reading this—if you like a girl, for crying out loud, just ask her out on a date. Don't be like, "Hey, do you want to hang out?" If you like a girl, ask her out on a date.)

So I kind of said all these words in a slightly nicer way to the guy. I was like, "You've got to ask her out." So a little while later, he said to me, "Guess what happened? I asked her out, and she said yes." And I'm like, "Of course she did. That's why she's been studying with you for the last year and a half."

For that couple, that was the season for starting. A lot of us have known this. We've experienced the start of a relationship, and that's wonderful. It's awesome. It's where you're like, "I can't believe it. I have butterflies everywhere in my body." But we also know that if we're going to grow, we need to make an effort to continue.

> IF WE'RE GOING TO GROW, WE NEED TO MAKE AN EFFORT TO CONTINUE.

We need to embrace the season of continuing because it's in the season of continuing that personal relationships either thrive or they die. Because once we've started, we have to continue the battle.

A BATTLE FOR YOUR HEART

When it comes to our relationship with Jesus, it's the same thing. I know this: you're reading this book because you have a personal relationship with God or you want one. You do. You've started that or you want to start it. But once you've started, you're in the season of continuing. You're in the season of continuing the battle.

The season of continuing is a season of battle. It's a battle for your heart.

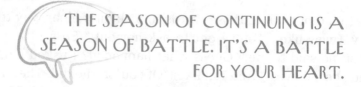

THE SEASON OF CONTINUING IS A SEASON OF BATTLE. IT'S A BATTLE FOR YOUR HEART.

Once you've started prayer because you want a personal relationship with God, what happens when it gets hard? What happens when prayer becomes a battle? What happens when your relationship with Jesus actually becomes a battle for your heart?

The *Catechism of the Catholic Church* talks about this. It has four sections. There's one on the creed, on the sacraments, on the commandments, and—my personal favorite—a section on prayer. And my favorite part within that section is on "the battle of prayer." You should totally check it out. One of the things it says is that "prayer is both a gift of grace and a determined response on our part" (CCC 2725). It's a gift of grace. So that means God does it; he's the giver of the gift. He invites us to this prayer. And prayer is a determined response on our part. We have to fight to do it. I love the next line: "Prayer always presupposes effort."

Prayer is a battle. It always presupposes effort.

"PRAYER ALWAYS PRESUPPOSES EFFORT"

(CCC 2725).

Now, why is this important to me? It's important to me because I started praying when I was fifteen years old, and I had read all these stories about these saints who would go in front of the Blessed Sacrament and kneel down to pray, and their hours of prayer would feel like minutes to them. So I thought that's what I would do. I would go in front of the Eucharist and kneel down in front of the tabernacle. And so I did it. I knelt down, and minutes felt like hours to me. And I remember thinking, "Am I doing something wrong? Because this is hard."

When I started praying, I thought that prayer would be like slipping into a hot tub, you know, because that's how people sometimes describe it. People describe prayer like you just ease into prayer and just rest in the Lord's presence. And I was like, "This is great. I love hot tubs." I thought I was going to get into the prayer like I was just easing into a hot tub, and I was going to relax and just let the Lord speak. We talked about how the first step of prayer is knowing God loves you and the second step is letting him love you. I thought that letting him love me would be like slipping into the hot tub, that the radiation of the Lord's presence would be like warm water.

I found, however, that prayer actually wasn't like that. And so when I came upon this teaching in the Catechism, I was like, "Oh, it's supposed to be a battle?" Sometimes continuing is awesome and beautiful and you get to slip into the warm hot tub. But mostly it involves effort. The season of continuing is the season of battling. I realized that actually prayer is less like slipping into a hot tub and more like jumping in the pool and doing laps.

Again, prayer is a gift of grace, and it presupposes effort. Here's the analogy. Prayer is a gift of grace so it's like the water in the pool. It can lift you up; it can give you buoyancy; it can cool you off. But if you're going to do laps, it always presupposes effort. When we recognize that, we can recognize that we're not doing something wrong. The fact that continuing in prayer is a battle does not necessarily mean that you're doing something wrong. Prayer always presupposes effort.

MATURITY

That recognition was such a huge thing for me. Let's go back to St. Paul's letter to the Philippians. St. Paul says that he continues, but why does he continue? He says, "Let those of us who are mature be thus minded" (Philippians 3:15). He continues because he wants maturity. And the reason why prayer is a battle is because God wants maturity for us, and maturity always passes through the desert. This concept is important: maturity always passes through dryness and difficulty.

> MATURITY ALWAYS PASSES THROUGH DRYNESS AND DIFFICULTY.

This is just the worst news but it's also the best news. It's bad news because it means that prayer is a battle, it's not a hot tub. But it's the best news because it means that you're not necessarily doing something wrong if you're being faithful to prayer and prayer feels like a total drag for days or weeks or months. Because maturity always passes through dryness and difficulty. Maturity always passes through a desert. It's necessary.

St. Teresa of Calcutta in 1947 had this incredible grace. For a whole year, her prayer was like consolation. It was like the hot tub. She would see Jesus in her prayer, and he would talk to her out loud in her prayer. Jesus asked her to start a new religious community, and it must have felt easy for her to say yes. But then from 1948 until the day she died, 50 years later, she entered into the desert, into dryness.

Every one of us experiences dryness in prayer. If I could ask how many people reading this have experienced this dryness in prayer, probably all of you would raise your hands. You're going to experience this at some point in your life. And you have to, because God wants to make you into a mature Christian.

So here are the questions we need to ask ourselves if we're in the middle of a desert. When we're experiencing dryness, our first question is, "What did I do wrong?" That's where we need to start, because we need to know whether we did something that caused this dryness, or whether this dryness is from God. And so the first question we have to ask when we're experiencing dryness is, "Am I aware of mortal sin?" No? OK. Are you conscious of any way that you've intentionally taken your heart and given it to something else? No? Well, then it's God who led you into this desert.

PURIFYING LOVE

Why does God lead you into the desert? Because the desert purifies your heart. When you show up to pray and you do not feel anything, you are in the place where saints are made.

WHEN YOU SHOW UP TO PRAY AND YOU DO NOT FEEL ANYTHING, YOU ARE IN THE PLACE WHERE SAINTS ARE MADE.

This is what happens. If you're anything like me, you'll recognize this. I have a mercenary heart. C.S. Lewis talked about this.[5] Having a mercenary heart means loving whoever is the highest bidder. Whoever's going to treat me the best, I give my heart to. But I don't want to just have a mercenary heart; I want to have a lover's heart. How do we get a lover's heart? Our hearts have to be purified, so we choose Jesus for his sake, not for what he gives us. Jesus has to lead us into the desert, so we choose him for his sake.

Another way to say it is that we have a prostitute's heart. I know that idea may seem alarming, but it comes from the Bible. Think about the book of Hosea in the Old Testament.

Hosea was called to be a prophet, not just with his words but with his life. And so here's what God asked. Hosea had to reflect the Lord God's faithfulness to Israel, even though Israel was unfaithful to God. And so God says to him in Hosea 1:2-3: "Go, take to yourself a wife of harlotry and have children of harlotry, for the land commits great harlotry by forsaking the LORD." And here's the thing: God tells Hosea she's not going to be faithful to you, but you need to be faithful to her.

So Hosea takes Gomer as his wife, and she will give her heart to any lover who pays for it: "For she said, 'I will go after my lovers, who give me my bread and my water, my wool and my flax, my oil and my drink'" (Hosea 2:5). She thinks those lovers would give her anything. Even though she's married to Hosea, even though he wants her heart just for himself, she says, "No, I'll go to whoever is the highest bidder."

Then, through the Lord's voice, Hosea has to say he's going to take away all these blessings, all these good things that give Gomer consolation. The Lord, through Hosea, says, "I will put an end to all her mirth, her feasts, her new moons, her sabbaths ...

And I will lay waste her vines and her fig trees" (Hosea 2:11-12). Basically, he brings an end to all these good things she enjoyed. And it's not because she's so bad, or that she's not worth loving. He takes these things away because it will purify her heart. "She shall pursue her lovers, but not overtake them; and she shall seek them, but shall not find them" (Hosea 2:7).

So what will happen? Through Hosea, the Lord says, "I will allure her, and bring her into the wilderness, and speak tenderly to her" (Hosea 2:14). This is God speaking to your heart whenever you experience dryness in prayer. It's God saying, "I will allure you, and I will lead you into the desert. And there I will speak to your heart." This is why God leads us into the desert. It's why we have to go into the dryness: so we realize that those things that we think will make us happy don't make us happy. Those things are not what our hearts were made for. Prayer is a battlefield for the heart.

When God speaks to our hearts in that desert place where we don't feel anything, our hearts get purified. Our loves get purified. That's important because not only does our knowledge of God need to be purified, but our love for God needs to be purified.

So many of us love God like a little kid loves her mom and dad. That is not a bad thing, but think about it. As a little kid, I would say I love my mom and dad because they give me stuff. I love my mom and dad because I feel a lot of affection for them. But if you're going to have the ability to love your parents for themselves, not just for their gifts, they have to take the gifts away.

So why does God lead us into the desert? Why does maturity pass through the desert and through dryness and difficulty? Because it has to. Because if God doesn't take away some of those things that make prayer easy, we will not love him for himself, and instead we'll just love the stuff he does for us.

So when you experience dryness, that doesn't mean you did something wrong. It means that God's saying, "Listen. I'm going to purify your heart. I'm going to let you love me for my own sake, not for the gifts that I give."

There's another reason why God leads us into the desert. I remember I read in a book by Fr. Jacques Philippe that God leads us into dryness, into the desert, not only so we can purify our hearts, but also so he can do surgery on our hearts. I recall Fr. Jacques Philippe says that dryness is God's anesthesia. God's plan for our heart is not just to mold it a little bit and kind of tweak it a little bit—God's plan for our heart is heart transplant stuff. God actually wants to give us a new heart. That's what Scripture says: "I will take out of your flesh the heart of stone and give you a heart of flesh" (Ezekiel 36:26).

Leading us into dryness is the way God gives us anesthesia, because this is going to be massive surgery. He's going to numb us up so that the heart transplant doesn't destroy us and so it doesn't make us flee from him. God gives us dryness and desert so he can do massive surgery, a heart transplant.

DISTRACTIONS

Part of the battle of prayer is dryness, and another part of the battle is distractions. I imagine again that everyone reading this has experienced distraction in prayer. All of us experience this, because it's just normal. For one, this is because our brains aren't static. Our brains are constantly moving, so it makes sense that you're going to think about something you want to pray about and all of a sudden, you're thinking about a thousand other things other than your prayer.

When we have distractions in prayer, a question we can ask is, Have I invited these distractions into my life? Did I do this to myself? Because sometimes we do that to ourselves. Here's a quick little example. I've mentioned before that years ago I did a thirty-day silent retreat. It changed my life, and it was amazing. It was powerful. But here's the embarrassing part of that. In the middle of that thirty-day silent retreat, one TV show that I was into came back on the air, and I didn't want to miss that episode. This was pre-DVR and pre-Netflix. And so in the middle of a thirty-day silent retreat, I snuck into the one room in the entire retreat center where they had a television set, and I turned it on and watched this TV show for an hour. (It was *Buffy the Vampire Slayer.* I'm so embarrassed!) I was thinking, "It's OK. I'm just taking a little one-hour break in these thirty days. Not a problem." But for the next five days I would try to go into prayer and I was totally distracted by the show's storyline. I was like, "Why did I just do this to myself?"

Sometimes, we do this, don't we? Right before we go into prayer, we feed our minds with all these different thoughts and therefore enter into prayer completely distracted. So one thing we can ask ourselves when we're battling with distraction in prayer is, "Wait, did I just do that to myself?"

When we're in prayer, and we're just constantly distracted, another question we can ask is, What do these distractions reveal? Maybe it's, "I'm very angry." Maybe I'm in prayer and I'm just so distracted by anger. This reveals something. I need to address this anger in my heart and bring it to Jesus. Or maybe in prayer I'm so worried and preoccupied and that's my distraction—I need to address that and bring it to Jesus. Sometimes, I'm so distracted because I'm really trying to avoid God's gaze. Why am I trying to avoid his gaze? Why am I trying to avoid him looking at me? What's going on?

So the next time you feel distracted in prayer, ask yourself, Have I brought this into my life? What do those distractions reveal?

DISCOURAGEMENT

In the battle of prayer, we have dryness, we have distractions, and we also have our own vulnerabilities. That's the third difficulty in prayer—our wounds.

I'm sure that a lot of us go to prayer and we're like, "God, I just I want you to take this problem away from me." Sometimes it's a physical wound. Sometimes we come to prayer and ask God to heal us from sickness. But sometimes it's a spiritual wound. Sometimes it's a persistent sin. I know so many of us struggle with these persistent sins that just keep coming back repeatedly. And we go to confession and we try to hand them over to the Lord, but then we go to prayer and they're still there. And we can be so discouraged. We have dryness, we have distraction, and we have discouragement.

But realize that sometimes God lets you endure the discouragement. He lets you live with the wounds. Why? Because sometimes, God wants your heart more than he wants your healing. And sometimes, it's those discouragements that lead you toward him more than ever. I know this because this is how God got my heart. It wasn't through my amazing awesomeness. I don't have amazing awesomeness. It wasn't through success or achievement. When I have success, God is the one who wins. It was through my wounds and through my being discouraged with my own wounds that God said, "I'm not going to give you healing. I don't want your healing as much as I want your heart."

And that's been my desert and part of my battle my whole life: God allowing me to experience certain wounds because he doesn't want my healing, he wants my heart. And I think many people can relate to that experience. When you have this persistent wound, whatever it is, you just really want it to be gone. St. Paul had a wound like this. And God says, "No, my grace is sufficient for you. You live with this wound because my power is made perfect in your weakness. I want your heart more than I want your healing" (see 2 Corinthians 12:9).

"[THE LORD] SAID TO ME, 'MY GRACE IS SUFFICIENT FOR YOU, FOR MY POWER IS MADE PERFECT IN WEAKNES'"

(2 Corinthians 12:9).

CONTINUING IN THE DESERT

These three elements of the desert are part of the battle of prayer. They are three elements of becoming a mature Christian: the dryness, the distractions, and the discouragement. I want to invite everybody to continue through the desert. I want to invite you to continue to battle to have a personal relationship with God. God himself will give you the love that you need to love him.

So often we think, "I just need to love him more." But no—God will give you the love that you need to love him back. He'll do it, but we need to continue that road through the desert, through dryness and distraction and discouragement. It is not my prayer that makes me holy. It's his love that makes me holy in the desert.

This is the only way. Jesus knew it—he spent forty days in the wilderness. The Israelites knew it—they spent forty years in the wilderness. All of the saints knew it. Mother Teresa knew it for fifty years in the wilderness. The wilderness, the desert, is where you become mature. The wilderness, the desert, is where you will be made into a saint. The wilderness, the desert, is where God leads you to win the battle for your heart.

Who is one person you know about, but don't actually know? Is Jesus one of those people for you?

What are some good ways to get to know Jesus, instead of just learning about him?

Have you thought of prayer as a battle before? Does thinking this way help you to understand its difficulties?

How can dedication to prayer help with dryness and distractions?

Have you experienced dryness or distractions in prayer? If so, what were some things that helped you in those seasons?

Did you know that saints experienced dryness and distractions in prayer, too? Does this change your perspective on those experiences? How did you first get to know about God? What were some of the first characteristics that you remember noting? Has your knowledge of God changed since then? How so?

In virtually everything, there is a season of "starting" and a season of "continuing." In relationships, the season of "continuing" is often more difficult. Would you describe your relationship with Christ as being in a season of starting or continuing?

Does knowing that dryness is an inevitable part of your prayer life help you persevere in prayer? If yes, why? If not, why not? What might help you begin to change the way that you perceive dryness?

Have you experienced distraction in prayer? When it comes to those distractions, do you notice them coming mostly from your inviting them in, or from somewhere else? What is the best strategy you've found for dealing with distractions?

Jesus sometimes wants your heart more than your healing. Does that thought encourage you, or does that thought dishearten you? What is encouraging? What is discouraging?

ACT

Keep persevering in your fifteen daily minutes of prayer. If this has been difficult for you, make a new plan for when and where you'll pray. Don't forget that God is listening, whether you feel it or not, even in dryness and distraction!

Chapter 5

YOUR STORY

As Catholics, I think we all know the story of Our Lord's Passion. When we come to church on Palm Sunday or Good Friday, most of us know what story we are going to hear. We know we'll stand and read through the whole story of how Jesus was arrested and condemned and crucified. We know what story to expect.

But that's our problem, a lot of times. We show up, and we know what story we're going to hear. We're used to it. We don't realize that this story is actually not just his story. This is actually our story.

MY STORY

Here's what I mean. I've been watching these videos of marriage proposals lately. There's one where this guy and girl were hanging out, and the guy started taking a video because he knew what was going to happen. All of a sudden this flash mob comes on with the Bruno Mars song "Marry You." And the girl's like, "Oh wow, that's awesome." That's when the guy jumps in and starts dancing to the song, too, and she's like, "What? He's part of the dance?" And then as the song unfolds she realizes, "Wait, he's singing to me. This song is about me. It's not just a cool thing—the whole song was for me." Imagine watching that and realizing it's for you.

There's this commercial for gum. You'd think if there's something that's not going to get you to cry, it's a gum commercial. But this one is different—honestly this one does get me all choked up whenever I watch it. It's the story of this guy and girl's relationship. On their first date, she gives him some gum, so he opens it up and takes the gum and then draws a little picture of the first date on the back of the wrapper. On the next wrapper, he draws the first kiss. And he goes through the whole relationship. And then one day she goes into this art gallery and she sees all the drawings on the backs of the gum wrappers with all the moments from their dates. The guy is watching her walking around this room. As she looks at these drawings, she realizes, "Wait, this is our story." And then there's the picture of him getting down on one knee. She turns around and there he is, kneeling to propose. She walks in the art gallery to look at pictures but she realizes, "Wait, this is my story."

So often, we show up for Mass, and we hear someone else's story. But it is personal. This is your story. What we hear in the story of Jesus' passion and crucifixion is our story. In some ways, it's so profound and it's so amazing that it's like the proposal. This is how much God loves you. Isn't that incredible? It blows my mind.

WHAT WE HEAR IN THE STORY OF
JESUS' PASSION AND CRUCIFIXION
IS OUR STORY.

BROKEN HEARTS

But also there's another piece. We can be convicted by this story. This story can break our hearts when we hear it and don't realize it's our story.

I'm thinking about King David. He was an Old Testament king, but he didn't always do great things. In fact, in 2 Samuel chapter 11, we see King David have a really bad time. He takes another man's wife as his lover. He gets her pregnant and then has her husband killed to avoid being in trouble. In the next chapter, what happens is that David thinks he's gotten past this. David thinks he escaped all punishment.

Then the prophet Nathan goes to David and says, "You need to judge this case for me. Here's what happened somewhere in your kingdom. There was a man who had an abundance of flocks and herds. He had sheep and goats in abundance, but he had a neighbor who had this one little ewe lamb. And his neighbor loved this lamb. He shared the little food he had from his table, and he would sleep with this little lamb against his chest, and he loved this lamb. But the rich man had some guests come, and rather than go into his field and choose one of his flock to kill and eat, he went over to his neighbor's house and he took his one little lamb that he had loved. He took it from his arms and he slaughtered it and he fed his friends with that other man's lamb. What should happen there?" (See 2 Samuel 12:1-4.)

I love David's response. He grew angry with that and he said to Nathan, "As the Lord lives, the man who has done this deserves to die; and he shall restore the lamb fourfold, because he did this thing, and because he had no pity" (2 Samuel 12:5-6). And then Nathan looks at David and he says four words: "You are the man" (2 Samuel 12:7).

Now, David heard a story about this other guy and was like, "That's terrible." And all of a sudden, Nathan said, "No, that's your story, David. You could have had any woman in this kingdom you possibly wanted. Uriah had one wife that he just loved with everything he had, and you took her from him." And in that moment, David hears this story and realizes, "Wait a second—that's my story." Sometimes the realization that the story is our story can be a moment like a proposal, and sometimes it can be this heartbreaking and crushing recognition of what we've done.

Do we recognize our story when we hear the Passion? This is not just someone else's story—this is our story. For some of us it's a proposal, but for others of us it's heartbreaking, because we played a part in the story. I'm sure a lot of you have seen the movie *The Passion of the Christ*, which recounts on film the story we read on Palm Sunday. Mel Gibson produced it, and he actually makes an appearance in his own movie. But you can only see his hands in his movie. It's his hands that drive the nails into Jesus' hands and feet. That's the only appearance that Mel Gibson makes, and he said it's because that's the only contribution he had to the story.

Yes, it's completely personal. But the only part that I contributed to this whole story is that I drove in the nails and I crucified my God.

THE STORY OF THE CRUCIFIX

When we realize that this is our story, it can be heartbreaking. In fact, one of my heroes is named Archbishop Fulton Sheen, and he says that everyone has an autobiography. He gave a talk, which I'll paraphrase here: "I think you have an autobiography as well," he said while holding up a crucifix. "This is your autobiography. This is my autobiography. I wrote this. This is my story, the story of my life, that I wrote.

The canvas to write my story was the flesh of my God, Jesus, and the pen I used to write was the lashes and the nails. The ink to write my story—the story of my life—was his blood. Everything in my life is written here. For as often as I reached out to take something that didn't belong to me, I nailed his hands to the Cross, so he couldn't reach out and take anything he wanted. For as often as I kind of crowned myself and said, 'You know I'm going live my own prideful life. I'm going to do my own thing in vanity,' I put a crown of thorns on my God, on my King. For as often as I went off and lived my own life—as often as I walked one way even though I knew God wanted me to live another way—I fixed his feet to the Cross so he could not go anywhere. That's my story. That's my life. This is my autobiography.

As often as I gossiped, I punched him in the mouth and his lips swelled so he couldn't speak. For as often as I lusted after someone, was willing to use someone for their appearance and look at their bodies and objectify them, my God was stripped naked in front of every person. That's my story. This is my autobiography. This is what I've written."

Archbishop Sheen said, "This is what I've done, but the other part is his contribution: he let me do it, in order to save my life."[6]

A LOVE STORY

Like the woman in that proposal video, and like King David, we realize that this is our story. It is awesome like a proposal, and it is also crushing and heartbreaking. This is the story that we wrote, and this is the story that God wrote. It's deeply personal because the point of the story is how to grow in love.

The point of recognizing that this is our story is not just to make us feel sad, not just to make us feel guilty. The whole point is to take it personally so you and I know how to grow in love. That is the reason to pray: to grow in love for God.

How do we take it personally so that we're not just feeling badly? How do we take it personally so that we get close to him? How do we get close to the God who loves us? Every prayer that you and I pray is a good prayer or a bad prayer depending on one thing: does this prayer help me love him better or does it not help me love him better?

We've talked about the two steps in prayer, recognizing that God loves you, and just letting him love you. We talked about how we have faith that he's present and then we just have to show up too and be present as well. We talked about how we enter into God's presence with fear but also that we can stay in his presence with fearlessness. We talked about what to do when prayer is dry, what to do when prayer is distracted and difficult. It is all personal. It is all so that we can love him more.

WATCH JESUS

Here, at the end, I want to share something with you that will change your life. If you get all those four things correct—that God loves you, that he's faithful, that he's fearful but also you can be fearless, and that we persevere in dryness—then if you do this next thing, I promise you, your life will change. It changed my life.

When I went into the seminary, I'd been praying for years by that point, but I still don't think I knew Jesus. I knew about Jesus, I knew about God, but I don't think I really knew him. And so this priest at the seminary said, "I think you should go on a thirty-day silent retreat." I talked about this, and I mentioned that it changed my whole entire life, but I want to tell you why. It was because of the way I prayed. I want to share with you the way I prayed. If you pray like this, I'm telling you, it will change your life.

It's been twenty years, and the gift that God gave me from that time has not stopped. And that gift is that I have never doubted Jesus for all these years. It was his grace and completely his gift. Even if things crashed around me, I never doubted, because of his grace and his gift. I never faltered, even when my life was a wreck. Even when I was crashing down into the sewers, Jesus gave me this trust in him, and I want you to have that same trust.

Here's how I prayed, and here's how I'm inviting you to pray this week and maybe for the rest of your life. In Philippians chapter 2, it says this: that though Jesus was in the form of God, he humbled himself and became a human being. He became like us, and that gives us one of the great secrets of prayer. If you don't know how to pray, pray with Jesus's humanity. Now, that sounds really technical, but here's what it means. It means open up the Gospels and watch Jesus.

> IF YOU DON'T KNOW HOW TO PRAY, OPEN UP THE GOSPELS AND WATCH JESUS.

I invite you to do this all week. Open up the Gospels and watch Jesus. This type of prayer was developed or invented by a man named Ignatius of Loyola, founder of the Jesuits, and it involves all five senses. It involves your imagination.

Read a passage of Scripture and just take out a small scene to focus on. The story of Jesus' passion is a good place to start. What I want to focus on right here is when Jesus goes into the garden of Gethsemane. It's a scene that we all know. And what Ignatius said to do is to use your imagination. Because what we do typically is we just read it without really slowing down: "Oh, he went to the garden of Gethsemane. He started praying, and then he got arrested, and so on." We just move on. Ignatius says, "Stop. Use your imagination."

Jesus was in the garden; what's the garden look like? Ignatius says to use your first sense: your sense of sight. Look around. Where's Jesus? Look for him in the garden. Is he kneeling? Is he flat on his face? What kind of clothes is he wearing? Luke says that he was so grieved that his sweat became like drops of blood on the ground. Can you see that trickling of the sweat, of the blood off of his face, soaking his clothes? Look around. Can you see the other apostles? What are they doing? See where they're standing? See where they're sitting? They're falling asleep. You know this already. So just look around.

The second thing to do is to add a second sense: sound. Can you hear Jesus groaning from the depths of his heart? Can you hear the apostles snoring? Can you hear the crickets? It's the middle of the night. Can you hear the bullfrogs? What do you hear? Do you hear the breeze in the trees? Just listen.

Next, you can add the sense of feeling, so you can feel that breeze against your skin. It's a cool breeze because it's the middle of the night. Can you feel that breeze against your skin as you watch Jesus as he's weeping and sweating blood and groaning in agony, and the apostles are snoring quietly off to the side?

What's it smell like? You're in the garden of olives. Can you smell those trees? Can you smell those leaves opening up and feeding their fragrances to the wind?

Can you even taste in your mouth? You just had this lamb supper, you just had this Passover meal. Can you still taste a little bit of that lamb or those bitter herbs?

And here you are with Jesus. Now, here's what happens. This is what happens every single time, if you pray like this. It changes everything. Why? Because you get to know who Jesus is. It doesn't have anything to do with thoughts or creative ideas. What it has to do with is just being able to love him. I'm inviting you to do this once a day this whole week. Pick a scene from the Passion and just watch Jesus. Listen to what you hear. Smell what it smells like.

If you need to, you can interact with the people in the Gospel scene. I know some of you would do this. If you were there, you'd get down on your knees next to Jesus, and you'd just want to put your hand on his shoulder. I know some of you would want to get down right next to him and grab both of his shoulders with your hands and draw them to your chest.

Others of you would go to the apostles and kick them awake and say, "What are you doing? This is your Lord. He's going to die right now." So do that in your prayer. See Peter take out his sword.

I promise you, if you do this, if you pray like this, the day's going to come years from now when you say, "Man, ever since I started praying like this, my life has never been the same. I don't just know *about* Jesus—I *know* him. I don't just love the idea of Jesus—I *love* him."

LOVE

The whole point is love. The point of praying is not stringing together beautiful ideas. It's not having great insight into God. It's not just knowing more about God. The test of all of our prayers is this: does this help me grow in love, or doesn't it?

Remember Thérèse? I mentioned her before. She is a great saint. The last few years of her life, she was sick with tuberculosis, and she only was able to use half of one lung to breathe for the last months of her life. She talked about how painful it was. I bet it would be pretty uncomfortable. Imagine only being able to use one half of one lung for months at a time, not being able to sleep for more than three hours at a time, and hardly being able to think one thought. And her sisters said to her, "You seem like you're praying all the time." She said, "I *am* praying all the time."

Thérèse's sisters said to her, "But how can you focus? You're in so much pain." If you've ever been so heartbroken that you can't even think, you know what this feels like. Anyone in so much pain that you can't think great thoughts about God knows what this is like. Thérèse, this twenty-four-year-old girl, unable to breathe, unable to think, said, "I can't think at all. I can't even string two thoughts together, but I can love him. I lie here and I gasp for air and I let him love me."[7]

This is the secret of leaving the "it's nothing personal" kind of faith and realizing that this is your story. Everything we do here is your story. God doesn't need your great thoughts or your great accomplishments. All he wants is your heart.

GOD WANTS YOUR HEART.

REFLECT

Have you ever heard someone telling your story without knowing that it was you they were talking about? *(This could have been more negative, like gossip. Or it could have been positive, like sharing a cool story that they simply didn't realize was about you.) If you haven't, do you know anyone who has?*

Have you ever "gotten used to" the good news of what Christ has done for us? How can you make sure that you don't take it for granted?

Could you see yourself in David's place? What does it mean to you that the way we contribute to Christ's story is by nailing him to the Cross?

How can knowing how we fit into the gospel story help us to grow in love?

Archbishop Sheen's reflection on the crucifix is a powerful one. In what other ways is a person's story "written" upon the body of Christ on the Cross?

The test of whether mental prayer is good is whether this or that grows, strengthens, or fosters love. Are you aware of any times you have done a kind of mental prayer that didn't seem fruitful (in increasing love) at first, but then became so?

Have you ever practiced *Ignatian Prayer? What was it like? If it was difficult for you, what were some of the obstacles that you found? If it was a good experience, can you describe some of the fruits from it or why it was a good experience?*

When it comes to *Ignatian Prayer, are there some scenes or events from the Gospels that you have found easier to pray with than others?* (For example, I know for me personally, I've always found it more difficult to pray with the Passion than any other scene. I think that it is because I keep feeling pressure to "feel" something. I can engage much more easily in almost every other Gospel scene.)

ACT

This week*, ask the Holy Spirit to help you engage the Gospel stories (your stories!) with your imagination. Read a passage in which Jesus is interacting with others, and then close your eyes and imagine the scene. If you like, add your senses to your prayer.*

REMEMBER

- The whole plan of God is to bring us into personal relationship, but for so many of us, "it's nothing personal." To take it personally, so our faith goes right to our hearts, we need to pray.

- Prayer is not a technique. There are two steps to coming to prayer. Step one: Recognize God loves you. Step two: Let God love you.

- To take prayer personally, there are two more steps. Step one: Have faith that God is present. Step two: Show up to prayer with faithfulness.

- To have a personal relationship with God, we need to let God be God. We enter into God's presence with fear, but we can stay in his presence with fearlessness.

- When we come to know Jesus, our knowledge is purified, but our love needs to be purified, too. God leads us into the desert where prayer is a battle. We battle with dryness, distraction, and discouragement in prayer so that we learn to love him for himself.

- The story of the Cross is our story. It is awesome like a proposal, and it is also heartbreaking. If we watch Jesus in the Gospels, we will get to know him and grow in love. God wants our hearts.

NOTES

1   Pew Research Center's Forum on Religion and Public Life, "U.S. Religious Landscape Survey," 2008, available at religions. pewforum.org.

2   St. Hilary of Poitiers, *Treatise on the Psalms, Ps 127, 1-3; (CSEL 24, 628-630).*

3   See David Lewis, "St. Teresa of Avila," EWTN, available at ewtn.com.

4   Author's paraphrasing of St. Thérèse of Lisieux, *Story of a Soul: The Autobiography of Saint Thérèse of Lisieux*, 3rd ed., trans. John Clarke, (Washington, DC: ICS Publications, 1996).

5   See, for example, C.S. Lewis, "As the Ruin Falls."

6   Author's paraphrasing of "The Crucifixion and the Meaning of the Resurrection" from Fulton Sheen's lessons on Holy Week, available at fultonsheen.com.

7   Author's paraphrasing.

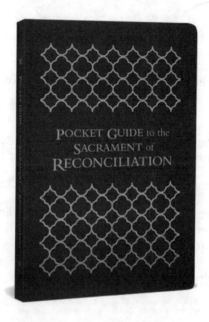